Alfred's Easy ukulele songs

CLASSIC ROCK

50 HITS OF THE '60s, '70s & '80s

Produced by
Alfred Music
P.O. Box 10003
Van Nuys, CA 91410-0003
alfred.com

WITHDRAWN

Printed in USA.

ISBN-10: 1-4706-3284-5
ISBN-13: 978-1-4706-3284-7

Cover Photos
Maestro Mango Tenor ukulele courtesy of Your Perfect Guitar, yourperfectguitar.com. Photographed by Arun Palaniappa

 Alfred Cares. Contents printed on environmentally responsible paper.

artist index

contents

TITLE	ARTIST	

STRUM PATTERNS

Below are a number of suggested patterns that may be used while strumming the chords for the songs in this book. Think of these as starting points from which you may embellish, mix up, or create your own patterns.

Note the markings above the staff that indicate the direction of the strums.

⊓ indicates a downstroke

∨ indicates an upstroke

BEHIND BLUE EYES

Use Suggested Strum Pattern #6
Moderately ♩ = 120

Words and Music by
PETER TOWNSHEND

Use Suggested Strum Pattern #2

Interlude:

Bridge:

When my fist clench - es, crack it o - pen, be - fore I use___ ___ it and lose___ my cool.___ When I smile___ tell___ me some bad___ ___ news be - fore I laugh___ and act like a fool.___

Use Suggested Strum Pattern #6

Behind Blue Eyes - 3 - 3

25 OR 6 TO 4

Words and Music by
ROBERT LAMM

Use Suggested Strum Pattern #6

Moderately fast ♩ = 146

25 or 6 to 4 - 2 - 1

BABY IT'S YOU

Use Suggested Strum Pattern #5

Moderately ♩ = 96

Words and Music by
BURT BACHARACH, MACK DAVID
and BARNEY WILLIAMS

Verse:

1. It's not the way you smile that___ touched my___ heart.
2. Is it true what they say a - bout you?_____

It's not the way___ you kiss that tears me a - part.___
They say you'll nev - er ev-er nev - er___ be true.___

Chorus:

1. Man - y, man - y, man - y nights go by,___ I sit a - lone___ at
2. It does - n't mat - ter what they say,___ I know I'm gon - na love you

home and cry_____ o - ver you. What can I do?___
an - y old way. What___ can I do___ with - out you?

Baby It's You - 2 - 1

BORN TO RUN

Words and Music by
BRUCE SPRINGSTEEN

Use Suggested Strum Pattern #1 or #6

Moderately ♩ = 138

Born to Run - 4 - 1

14

Verse 2:
Wendy, let me in, I wanna be your friend,
I want to guard your dreams and visions.
Just wrap your legs 'round these velvet rims
And strap your hands across my engines.
Together we could break this trap,
We'll run 'til we drop, baby, we'll never go back.
Will you walk with me out on the wire,
'Cause, baby, I'm just a scared and lonely rider.
But I gotta find out how it feels,
I want to know if love is wild, girl, I want to know if love is real.
(To Saxophone Solo:)

Verse 3:
The highway's jammed with broken heroes
On a last chance power drive.
Everybody's out on the run tonight but there's no place left to hide.
Together, Wendy, we can live with the sadness,
I'll love you with all the madness in my soul.
Someday, girl, I don't know when, we're gonna get to that place
Where we really want to go and well walk in the sun.
But 'til then, tramps like us, baby, we were born to run.
Ah, honey, tramps like us, baby, we were born to run.
Come on with me, tramps like us, baby, we were born to run.
(To Outro:)

CAN'T YOU SEE

Use Suggested Strum Pattern #4

Words and Music by
TOY CALDWELL

Moderately slow ♩ = 84

1. Gon - na take a freight train down at the sta - tion, Lord,___
2. *See additional lyrics*

I don't care where it goes.___

Gon - na climb a moun - tain, the high - est moun - tain,___

I jump off, no - bod - y gon - na know.___ Can't you see,___

Can't You See - 2 - 1

Verse 2:
I'm gonna buy a ticket now,
As far as I can, ain't never comin' back.
Grab me a southbound all the way to Georgia now,
'Til the train, it run out of track.
(To Chorus:)

Can't You See - 2 - 2

THE CHAIN

Use Suggested Strum Pattern #6

Moderately slow ♩ = 74

Words and Music by
LINDSEY BUCKINGHAM, CHRISTINE McVIE,
STEVIE NICKS, MICK FLEETWOOD and JOHN McVIE

The Chain - 3 - 1

COLOUR MY WORLD

Words and Music by
JAMES PANKOW

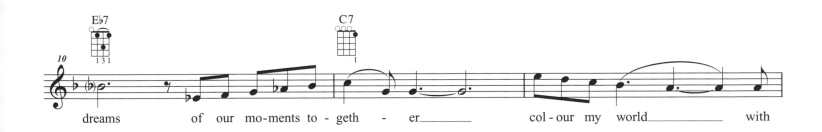

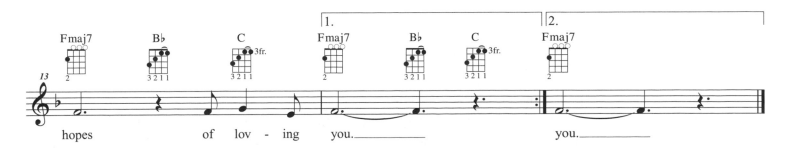

THE CIRCLE GAME

Use Suggested Strum Pattern #6
(See suggested picking pattern for Verses at bar 6)

Words and Music by
JONI MITCHELL

The Circle Game - 2 - 1

Verse 2:
Then the child moved ten times 'round the seasons
Skated over ten clear, frozen streams
Words like "when you're older" must appease him
And promises of someday make his dreams
(To Chorus:)

Verse 3:
Sixteen springs and sixteen summers gone now
Cartwheels turn to carwheels through the town
And they tell him take your time, it won't be long now
Till you drag your feet to slow the circles down
(To Chorus:)

Verse 4:
So the years spin by and now the boy is twenty
Though his dreams have lost some grandeur coming true
There'll be new dreams, maybe better dreams, and plenty
Before the last revolving year is through
(To Chorus:)

DANCING IN THE DARK

Words and Music by
BRUCE SPRINGSTEEN

Use Suggested Strum Pattern #1

Moderately fast ♩ = 144

1. I get up in the eve - ning,____ and I ain't____ got noth - in' to say.

2.3. *See additional lyrics*

I come home in the morn - ing; I go to bed feel - ing the____ same way.

____ I ain't noth-ing but tired.____ Man, I'm just tired____ and bored____ with my -

self. Hey, there, ba - by, I could use____ just a lit - tle help.

Chorus:

You can't start a fire,____ you can't start a fire____ with - out____ a spark.

____ This gun's for hire____ e - ven if we're just danc - ing in____ the dark.

Dancing in the Dark - 2 - 1

Verse 2:
Message keeps getting clearer;
Radio's on and I'm moving 'round the place.
I check my look in the mirror;
I wanna change my clothes, my hair, my face.
Man, I ain't getting nowhere just living in a dump like this.
There's something happening somewhere;
Baby, I just know there is.
(To Chorus:)

Verse 3:
Stay on the streets of this town
And they'll be carving you up all right.
They say you got to stay hungry;
Hey, baby, I'm just about starving tonight.
I'm dying for some action;
I'm sick of sitting 'round here trying to write this book.
I need a love reaction;
Come on now, baby, gimme just one look.
(To Chorus:)

DO YOU FEEL LIKE WE DO

Words and Music by
PETER FRAMPTON, JOHN SIOMOS,
RICK WILLIS and MICK GALLAGHER

Use Suggested Strum Pattern #6

Moderately ♩ = 106

Intro:

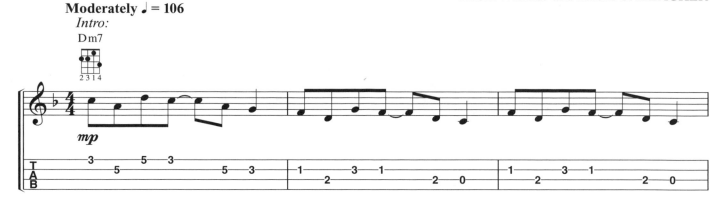

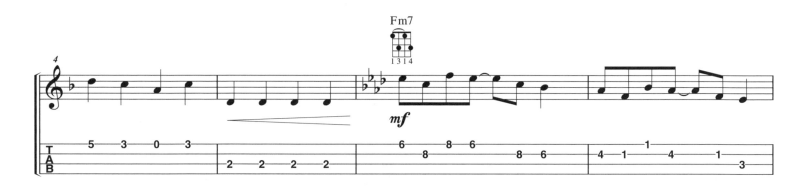

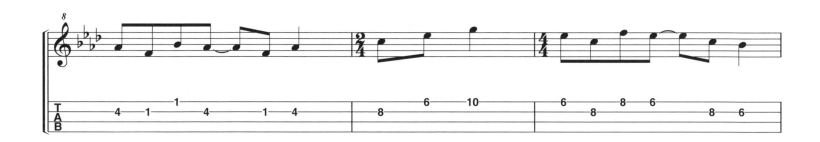

Do You Feel Like We Do - 2 - 1

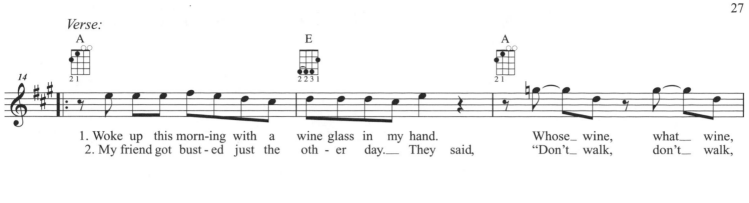

DO YOU WANT TO KNOW A SECRET

Use Suggested Strum Pattern #4
Slowly

Words and Music by
JOHN LENNON and
PAUL McCARTNEY

Intro:

You'll nev-er know how much I real-ly love you.

Moderately *Verse:*

You'll nev-er know how much I real-ly care. Lis-ten,

do you want to know a se-cret? do you prom-ise not to tell? Woah.

Clos-er, let me whis-per in your ear.

Say the words you long to hear. I'm in love with you, ooh. *To Coda*

1. **2.** *Bridge:*

I've known a se-cret for a week or two.

No-bod-y knows; just we two. *D.S. al Coda*

Coda

Ooh. Ooh. *rit.*

DON'T STOP BELIEVIN'

Use Suggested Strum Pattern #2

Words and Music by
JONATHAN CAIN, NEAL SCHON
and STEVE PERRY

Moderately

Intro:

Verse 1:

Just a small town girl,___ liv-in' in a lone-ly world.___

She took the mid-night train___ go-in' an-y - where.___

Just a cit-y boy,___ born and raised in South De-troit.___

He took the mid-night train___ go-in' an-y - where.___

FEELIN' STRONGER EVERY DAY

Use Suggested Strum Pattern #2

Moderately fast with a half-time feel ♩ = 160

Words and Music by
PETER CETERA and JAMES PANKOW

Feelin' Stronger Every Day - 3 - 1

Bridge:

Af -ter what__ you meant__ to__ me,__ ooh, ba - by,__ now,__

I can make__ it eas - i - ly.__ Yeah, yeah, yeah.

I know that__ we both__ a - gree,__ the best thing to hap-pen to you__

____ is the best thing that hap-pened to me,_____ Yeah, yeah,

*yeah.

*Sing first time only.

Chorus:

Feel - in' strong - er____ ev - 'ry day.__ You know I'm al - right__ now.__

Repeat and fade

__ Feel - in' strong - er____ ev - 'ry day.__ You know I'm al - right__ now.__

HOLD THE LINE

Use Suggested Strum Pattern #13
Or use Intro as a rhythm model throughout

Words and Music by
DAVID PAICH

Moderately ♩. = 98

1. It's not in the way_____ that you hold me,
2.3. It's not in the words_____ that you told me,

it's not in the way you_____ say you care.
it's not in the way you_____ say you're mine.

It's not in the way you've_ been treat - ing_____ my friends,
It's not in the way that_____ you came back_____ to me,

it's not in the way that_____ you stayed till_____ the end. }
it's not in the way that_____ your love set_____ me free. }

Hold the Line - 3 - 1

Coda

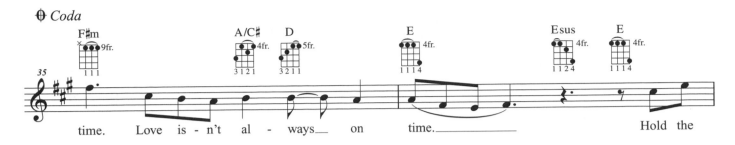

time. Love is - n't al - ways__ on time._____ Hold the

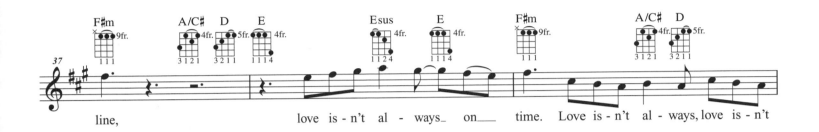

line, love is - n't al - ways_ on__ time. Love is - n't al - ways, love is - n't

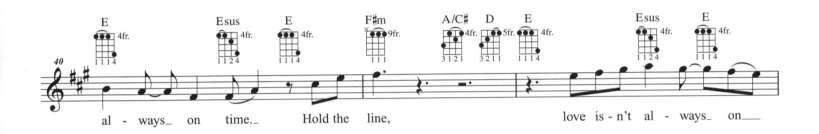

al - ways_ on time._ Hold the line, love is - n't al - ways_ on__

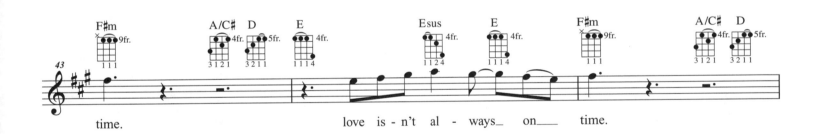

time. love is - n't al - ways_ on__ time.

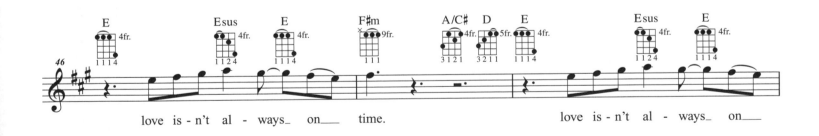

love is - n't al - ways_ on__ time. love is - n't al - ways_ on__

time. Whoa,__ whoa, whoa._____

Hold the Line - 3 - 3

GO YOUR OWN WAY

Use Suggested Strum Pattern #2
Moderately ♩ = 136

Words and Music by
LINDSEY BUCKINGHAM

1. Lov - ing you is - n't the right thing to do.
2. Tell me why ev - 'ry - thing turned a - round.

How can I ev - er change
Pack - ing up, shack - ing up's

things that I feel?
all you wan - na do.

If I could,
If I could,

ba - by, I'd give you my world.
ba - by, I'd give you my world.

How can I
O - pen up,

when you won't take it from me?
ev - 'ry - thing's wait - ing for you.

Go Your Own Way - 2 - 1

GOOD TIMES BAD TIMES

Words and Music by
JIMMY PAGE, JOHN PAUL JONES
and JOHN BONHAM

Use Suggested Strum Pattern #7

Good Times Bad Times - 2 - 1

HIT ME WITH YOUR BEST SHOT

Use Suggested Strum Pattern #1
or Rhythm indicated in Intro
Moderately ♩ = 128

Words and Music by
EDDIE SCHWARTZ

Intro:

Verses 1 & 2:

1. Well, you're a   real   tough   cook - ie   with   a   long   his - to - ry   of
2. *See additional lyrics*

break - ing   lit - tle   hearts   like   the   one   in   me.   That's   o - kay,   let's   see___

___ how   you   do___   it.   Put   up   your   dukes,___   let's   get   down   to___   it.

Chorus:

Hit   me   with   your   best   shot.   Why   don't   you   hit   me   with   your   best   shot?___

Hit   me   with   your   best   shot.   Fire___   a - way.___

2. You   Well, you're a

Hit Me with Your Best Shot - 2 - 1

43

Hit Me with Your Best Shot - 2 - 2

Verse 2:
You come on with a come on, you don't fight fair.
But that's okay, see if I care.
Knock me down, it's all in vain.
I'll get right back on my feet again.
(To Chorus:)

HOLD YOUR HEAD UP

Words and Music by
ROD ARGENT and CHRIS WHITE

**Use Suggested Strum Pattern #1
or Intro rhythm simile throughout**

Moderately ♩ = 96

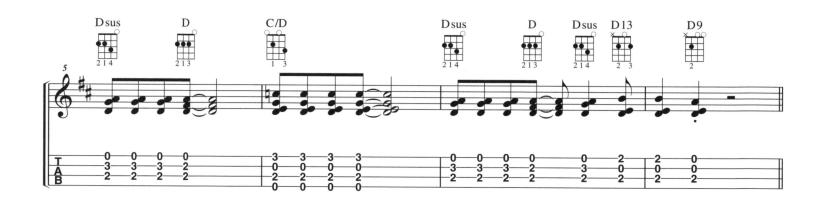

1. And if it's bad,___ don't let it get you down,___ you can take___ it.
2.3. And if they stare,___ just let them burn their eyes___ on your mov - ing.

And if it hurts,___ don't let them see you cry,___ you can make___
And if they shout,___ don't let it change a thing___ that you're do -

Hold Your Head Up - 2 - 1

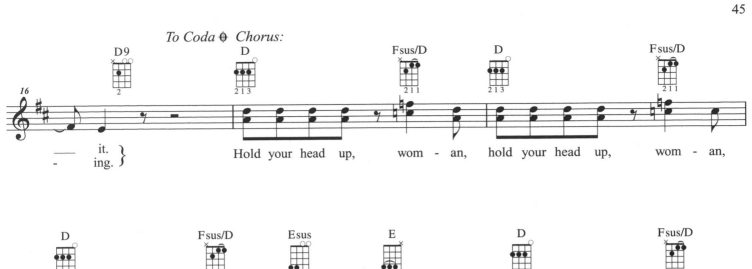

To Coda ⊕ *Chorus:*

Hold your head up, wom - an, hold your head up, wom - an,

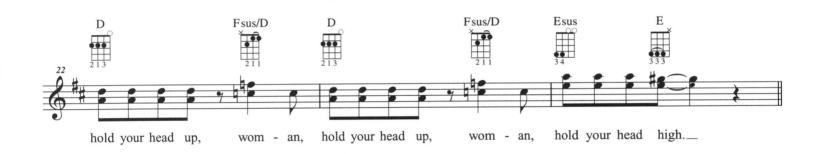

hold your head up, wom - an, hold your head high.___ Hold your head up, wom - an,

hold your head up, wom - an, hold your head up, wom - an, hold your head high.___

N.C.

1.   2.   *D.S. % al Coda*

⊕ *Coda*   *Repeat and fade*

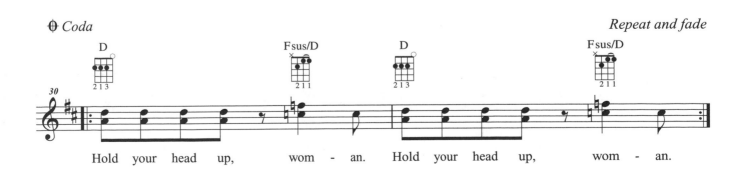

Hold your head up, wom - an. Hold your head up, wom - an.

Hold Your Head Up - 2 - 2

I HEAR YOU KNOCKING

Use Suggested Strum Pattern #1
or use Intro figure as rhythm pattern throughout
Moderately ♩ = 120

Words and Music by
DAVE BARTHOLOMEW
and PEARL KING

I Hear You Knocking - 2 - 1

I SAW HER STANDING THERE

Use Suggested Strum Pattern #1

Moderately fast

Words and Music by
JOHN LENNON and PAUL McCARTNEY

1. Well, she was

Verses 1 & 2:

just sev - en - teen,___ you know what I mean.___ And the
she looked at me,___ and I, I could see___ that be -

way she looked___ was way be - yond com - pare.___ } So
bore too long___ I'd fall in love with her.___ }

how could I___ dance with an - oth - er.___ Oh! When I

saw her stand - ing there.

|1.

2. Well,

|2.

Well, my

Bridge:

heart went boom___ when I crossed that room___ and I

LET'S SPEND THE NIGHT TOGETHER

Use Suggested Strum Pattern #1
Moderately ♩ = 120

Words and Music by
MICK JAGGER and KEITH RICHARDS

Intro:

Bah - ba dah - da, bop

bop ba dah dup. Bah - ba dah - da, bop bop ba dah dup.

Bah - ba dah - da, bop, bop. Bah - ba dah - da, bop bop ba dah dup.

Verse:

1. Don't you wor-ry 'bout what's on your mind,___ oh, my.___ (Bah - ba dah - da, bop,
2. I feel so strong___ that I can't dis - guise,___ oh, my.___ Let's___ spend the night
3. This does-n't hap-pen to me ev-'ry - day,___ oh, my.___ Let's___ spend the night

bop, ba dah dup.) I'm in no hur-ry, I can take my time,___ oh,
to - geth - er. But I just___ can't a - pol - o - gize,___ oh,
to - geth - er. No ex - cus-es of - fered an - y - way,___ oh,

my. (Bah - ba dah - da, bop, bop, ba dah dup.) I'm go - ing red___
no. Let's___ spend the night to - geth - er. Don't hang me up___
my. Let's___ spend the night to - geth - er. I'll sat - is - fy___

Let's Spend the Night Together - 3 - 1

Doo,_____ doo,_____ doo.   You know I'm smil - ing, ba - by.

You need some guid - ing, ba - by,   I'm just de - cid - ing, ba - by,

now,   I need you more___ than ev - er.   Let's spend the night___ to - geth - er.

Let's spend the night___ to - geth - er now.   Bah - ba dah - da,   bop,   bop.

D.S. % al Coda   *Coda*

Bah - ba dah - da, bop   bop ba dah dup.   to - geth - er now.__

___ (Bah - ba dah - da,   bop,   bop.)   (Bah - ba dah - da,   bop   bop ba dah dup.)

Repeat ad lib. and fade

Bah - ba dah - da,   bop,   bop.   (Bah - ba dah - da, bop   bop ba dah dup.)

Let's Spend the Night Together - 3 - 3

LIDO SHUFFLE

Words and Music by
BOZ SCAGGS and DAVID PAICH

Use Suggested Strum Pattern #1 (add a swing/shuffle feel)

Intro:
N.C.

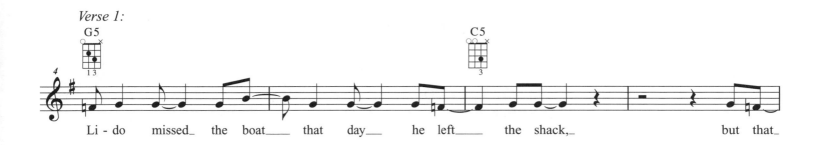

Verse 1:

Li - do missed the boat that day he left the shack, but that was all he missed, and he ain't com - in' back. 2. In a tomb-

Verses 2 & 3:

- stone bar in a juke joint car he made a stop just long

3. Li - do be run-nin' hav-in' great big fun 'til he got the note say-in', "Tow

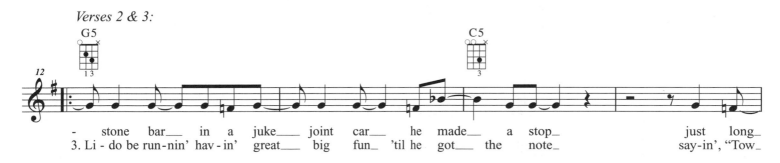

— e - nough to grab the han - dle off the top. Next

— the line or blow it," and that was all she wrote. He be mak-

Lido Shuffle - 3 - 1

ought to get it, one last shot 'fore we quit it, one more for

the road.

Li -

THE LETTER

Words and Music by
WAYNE CARSON THOMPSON

Use Suggested Strum Pattern #2

Moderately ♩ = 132

The Letter - 2 - 1

The Letter - 2 - 2

LIFE IN THE FAST LANE

Use Suggested Strum Pattern #6

Bright rock ♩ = 220 (with a half-time feel)

Words and Music by
DON HENLEY, GLENN FREY
and JOE WALSH

Life in the Fast Lane - 3 - 1

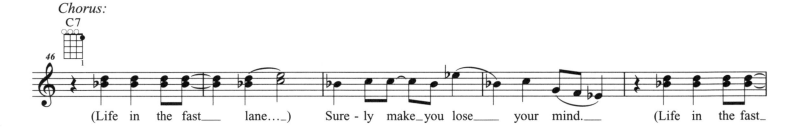

Verse 2:
Eager for action, and hot for the game.
The coming attraction, the drop of a name.
They knew all the right people, they took all the right pills,
They threw outrageous parties, they paid heavenly bills.
There were lines on the mirror, lines on her face.
She pretended not to notice, she was caught up in the race.
Out in the evening, until it was light,
He was too tired to make it, she was too tired to fight about it.
Surely make you lose your mind. Yeah.
(To Chorus:)

Verse 3:
Blowin' and burnin' blinded by thirst,
They didn't see the stop sign, took a turn for the worst.
She said, "listen, baby, you can hear the engine ring,
We've been up and down this highway,
Haven't seen a goddamn thing.
He said, "Call the doctor, I think I'm gonna crash."
"And, doctor say he's comin', but you got to pay him cash."
They went rushin' down that freeway, messin' 'round and got lost,
They didn't care, they were just dying to get off and it was…
(To Chorus:)

LIGHT MY FIRE

Use Suggested Strum Pattern #6
(See picking pattern for Verses at bar 6)

Moderately ♩ = 126

Words and Music by
THE DOORS

Light My Fire - 2 - 1

LOLA

Use Suggested Strum Pattern #6

Words and Music by
RAY DAVIES

Moderately bright (with a half-time feel) ♩ = 144

Lola - 4 - 1

Verse 4:

that's the way___ that I want it to stay___ and I_____ al-ways want it to

be that way___ for my Lo - la, Lo-Lo - Lo-Lo - Lo - la.

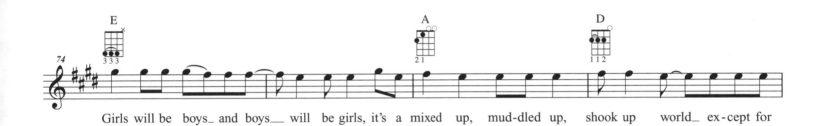

Girls will be boys_ and boys__ will be girls, it's a mixed up, mud-dled up, shook up world_ ex-cept for

D.S. ℅ *al Coda*

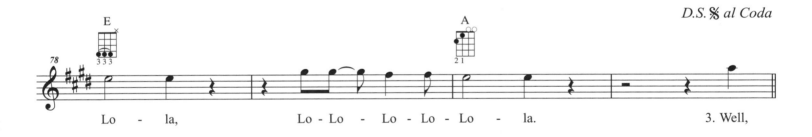

Lo - la, Lo-Lo - Lo-Lo - Lo - la. 3. Well,

⊕ *Coda*   *Outro:*

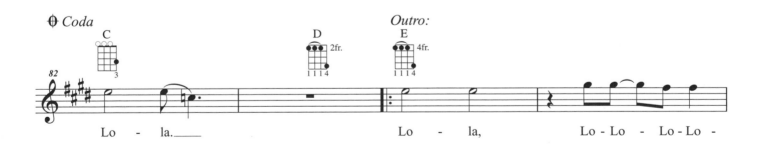

Lo - la.___ Lo - la, Lo-Lo - Lo-Lo -

Repeat and fade

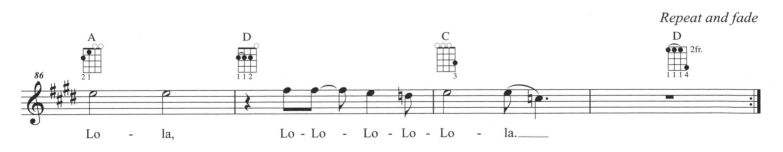

Lo - la, Lo-Lo - Lo-Lo - Lo - la.___

Lola - 4 - 4

MARRAKESH EXPRESS

Use Suggested Strum Pattern #7

Moderately fast ♩ = 108

Words and Music by
GRAHAM NASH

Verse 3:
Take the train from Casablanca going south,
Blowing smoke rings from the corners of my m-m-m-m-mouth,
Colored cottons hang in the air,
Charming cobras in the square,
Striped djellebas we can wear at home.
Well, let me hear you, now.
(To Chorus:)

ONLY WOMEN BLEED

Use Suggested Strum Pattern #1

Moderately slow ♩ = 80

Words and Music by
ALICE COOPER and DICK WAGNER

Intro:

mf
hold throughout

Verse:

1. Man got his wom-an   to take his seed.____
2. Man makes your hair____ grey,   he's your life's mis - take.____

He got the pow - er, oh,   she got the need.
All you're real - ly look - ing for's   an e - ven break.

She spends her life____ through   pleas-ing up her man.____
He lies right at____ you,   you know you hate this game.____

She feeds him din - ner or   an - y - thing____ she can.____
He slaps you once in a while and you   live and love____ in pain.____

Interlude:

Chorus:

OPEN ARMS

Use Suggested Strum Pattern #9

Words and Music by
JONATHAN CAIN and STEVE PERRY

Gently ♩ = 104

Verse:

1. Ly - ing_____ be - side_____ you, here in_____ the dark; feel - ing your
2. Liv - ing_____ with - out_____ you; liv - ing_____ a - lone, this emp - ty

heart beat with mine. Soft - ly_____ you whis - per,
house seems so cold. Want - ing_____ to hold you,

you're so_____ sin - cere. How could our love be so blind?_____ We
want - ing_____ you near; how much I want - ed you home._____ But

Open Arms - 2 - 1

OUR HOUSE

Use Suggested Strum Pattern #1
Moderately slow ♩ = 70

Words and Music by
GRAHAM NASH

Out House - 2 - 1

PAINT IT, BLACK

Words and Music by
MICK JAGGER and KEITH RICHARDS

Use Suggested Strum Pattern #1 (all downstrokes)
Freely

Moderately fast
Drums

Verse:

1.5. I see a red door, and I want it paint-ed black.__
2. I see a line of cars and they're all paint-ed black.__
3.4. *See additional lyrics*

No col-ors an-y-more,__ I want them to turn black.__
With flow-ers and my love__ both nev-er to come back.__

Bridge:

1.5. I see the girls walk by__ dressed in__ their sum-mer clothes,__
2. I see peo-ple turn their heads__ and quick-ly look__ a-way.__
3.4. *See additional lyrics*

I have to turn my head__ un-til__ my dark-ness goes.__
Like a new-born ba-by, it__ just hap-pens ev-'ry__ day.__

Paint It, Black - 2 - 1

Verse 3:
I look inside myself and see my heart is black.
I see my red door, I must have it painted black.

Bridge 3:
Maybe then I'll fade away and not have to face the facts.
It's not easy facing up when your whole world is black.

Verse 4:
No more will my green sea go turn a deeper blue.
I could not foresee this thing happening to you.

Bridge 4:
If I look hard enough into the setting sun,
My love will laugh with me before the mornin' comes.
(To Verse 5:)

PINBALL WIZARD

Use Suggested Strum Pattern #1

Words and Music by
PETER TOWNSHEND

Pinball Wizard - 2 - 1

RIDERS ON THE STORM

Use Suggested Strum Pattern #6

Moderately ♩ = 102

Words and Music by
THE DOORS

1.4. Ri - ders on the storm, ri - ders on the storm. In -

to this house we're born, in - to this world we're thrown. Like a

To Coda ⊕

dog with-out a bone, an act - or out on loan. Ri - ders on the storm. 2. There's a

Verses 2 & 3:

kill - er on the road; his brain is squirm-ing like a toad. Take
got - ta love your man. Girl, you got - ta - love your man.

a long hol - i - day; let your chil - dren play. If you
Take him by the hand; make him un - der - stand. The

Riders on the Storm - 2 - 1

give this man a ride, sweet fam - i - ly will die. Kill - er on the road.
world on you de-pends, our life will nev - er end. Got - ta love your man.

Interlude:

3. You

D.S. % al Coda

Coda

Ri - ders on the storm.____

Ri - ders on the storm.____

ROCK AND ROLL

Use Suggested Strum Pattern #1

Words and Music by
JIMMY PAGE, ROBERT PLANT,
JOHN PAUL JONES and JOHN BONHAM

Briskly ♩ = 170

Intro:

Verse:

been a long time since I rock and roll - ed._____
been a long time since the book of love._____
3. *See additional lyrics*

It's been a long time since I did the stroll._____
I can't count the tears of a life_____ with no love._____

Rock and Roll - 3 - 1

Outro:

Yeah___ hey, yeah,___ hey,

yeah,___ hey, yeah,___ hey.

Ooh, yeah. Ooh,___ yeah.___ Ooh, yeah.

Ooh,___ yeah.___ It's been a long time, been a long time, been a long

lone - ly, lone - ly, lone - ly, lone - ly, lone - ly time.

Verse 3:
Oh, it seems so long since we walked in the moonlight,
Making vows that just couldn't work right, ha-ha, yeah.
Open your arms, open your arms, open your arms.
Baby, let my love come running in.
Yes, it's been a long time, been a long time,
Been a long lonely, lonely, lonely, lonely, lonely time.
(To Outro:)

SHE'S NOT THERE

Use Suggested Strum Pattern #6
Moderately ♩ = 132

Words and Music by
ROD ARGENT

(I CAN'T GET NO) SATISFACTION

Use Suggested Strum Pattern #4

Moderately

Words and Music by
MICK JAGGER and KEITH RICHARDS

Verse 2:
When I'm watchin' my TV,
And a man comes on and tells me
How white my shirts can be,
But he can't be a man 'cause he doesn't smoke
The same cigarettes as me.
I can't get no, oh, no, no, no.
Hey, hey, hey, that's what I say.
(To Chorus:)

Verse 3:
When I'm ridin' 'round the world,
And I'm doin' this and I'm signin' that,
And I'm tryin' to make some girl
Who tells me, baby, better come back maybe next week,
'Cause you see I'm on a losin' streak.
I can't get no, oh, no, no, no.
Hey, hey, hey, that's what I say.
I can't get no…
(To Outro:)

(I Can't Get No) Satisfaction - 2 - 2

SEPARATE WAYS
(WORLDS APART)

Use Suggested Strum Pattern #5
Moderately ♩ = 132

Words and Music by
JONATHAN CAIN and STEVE PERRY

1. Here we stand,___ worlds a-part,___ hearts bro-ken in
2. Trou-bled times;___ caught be-tween___ con-fu-sion and

two, two,___ two.___
pain, pain,___ pain.___

Sleep-less nights;___ los-ing ground,___ I'm reach-ing for
Dis-tant eyes;___ pro-mis-es___ we made___ were in

you, you,___ you.
vain, in vain,___ in vain.___

Feel-in' that it's
If you must___

Pre-chorus:

gone___ can change___ your mind. If we can't go
go,___ I wish___ you love. you'll nev-er walk a-

Separate Ways (Worlds Apart) - 4 - 1

SHE LOVES YOU

Words and Music by
JOHN LENNON and PAUL McCARTNEY

Use Suggested Strum Pattern #2
Moderately bright

She Loves You - 2 - 1

Verse 2:
She said you hurt her so she almost lost her mind.
But now she says she knows you're not the hurting kind.
She said she loves you and you know that can't be bad.
Yes, she loves you and you know you should be glad, oo.
(To Chorus:)

Verse 3:
You know it's up to you, I think it's only fair.
Pride can hurt you too, apologize to her.
Because she loves you and you know that can't be bad.
Yes, she loves you and you know you should be glad, oo.
(To Chorus:)

SPACE ODDITY

Use Suggested Strum Pattern #6
or Continue Intro Pattern Simile

Words and Music by
DAVID BOWIE

Space Oddity - 3 - 1

SPIRIT IN THE SKY

Use Suggested Strum Pattern #1

Moderately ♩ = 124

Words and Music by
NORMAN GREENBAUM

1. When I die and they lay me to rest,___ gon-na go___ to the place___ that's the best.
2.3. *See additional lyrics*

When I lay me down___ to die, go-in' up___ to the spir - it in the sky.

Go-in' up___ to the spir - it in the sky,___ that's where I'm gon-na go___ when I die.___

When I die and they lay me to rest,___ I'm gon-na go to the place___ that's the best.

Spirit in the Sky - 3 - 1

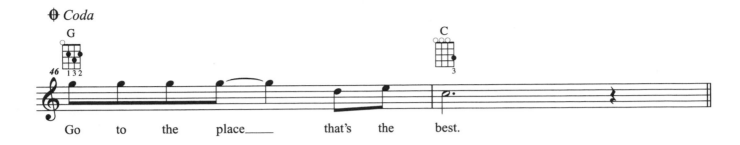

Go   to   the   place_____   that's   the   best.

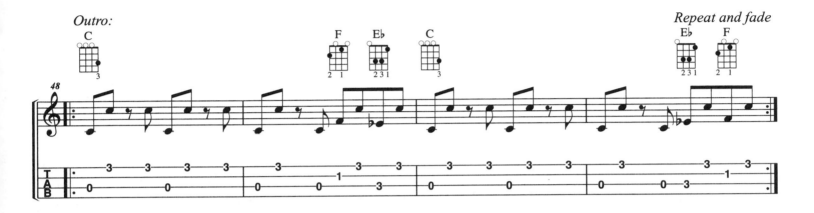

Verse 2:
Prepare yourself, you know it's a must,
Gotta have a friend in Jesus.
So you know that when you die,
He's gonna recommend you to the spirit in the sky.
Gonna recommend you to the spirit in the sky,
That's where you're gonna go when you die.
When you die and they lay you to rest,
You're gonna go to the place that's the best.

Verse 3:
Never been a sinner, I never sinned,
I got a friend in Jesus.
So you know that when I die,
He's gonna set me up with the spirit in the sky.
Oh, set me up with the spirit in the sky,
That's where I'm gonna go when I die.
When I die and they lay me to rest,
I'm gonna go to the place that's the best.
Go to the place that's the best.

STAIRWAY TO HEAVEN

(Excerpt)

Use Suggested Strum Pattern # 3

Slowly ♩ = 72

Intro:

Words and Music by
JIMMY PAGE and ROBERT PLANT

There's a

Stairway to Heaven (Excerpt) - 2 - 1

TEACH YOUR CHILDREN

Use Suggested Strum Pattern #6
Moderately bright ♩ = 78

Words and Music by
GRAHAM NASH

Verse 1:
You who are on the road___ must have a code that you can live by. And so, be - come_ your - self, be - cause_ the past___ is just a good - bye.

Chorus:
1. Teach your chil - dren_ well, their fa - ther's hell did slow - ly go___ by.___
2. Teach your par - ents_ well, their chil - dren's hell will slow - ly go___ by.___

And feed them on_ your dreams, the one_ they picked, the one_you'll know_ by.___

TELL HER NO

Use Suggested Strum Pattern # 6

Moderately fast ♩ = 134

Words and Music by
ROD ARGENT

Tell Her No - 2 - 1

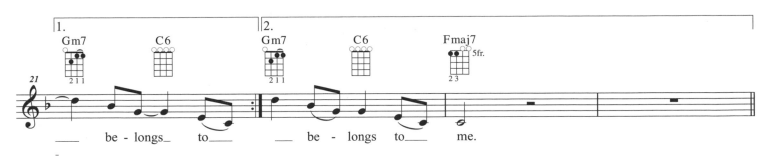

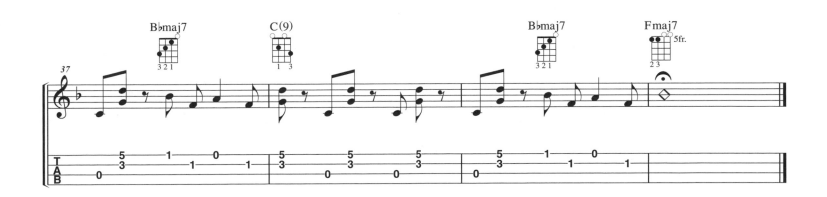

Tell Her No - 2 - 2

TIME OF THE SEASON

Use Suggested Strum Pattern #4

Moderately ♩ = 116

Words and Music by
ROD ARGENT

Time of the Season - 2 - 1

WASTED ON THE WAY

Use Suggested Strum Pattern #2
Moderately ♩ = 75

Words and Music by
GRAHAM NASH

Wasted on the Way - 2 - 1

Verse 2:
Oh, when you were young, did you question all the answers?
Did you envy all the dancers who had all the nerve?
Look around you now, you must go for what you wanted.
Look at all my friends who did and got what they deserved.
(To Chorus:)

Wasted on the Way - 2 - 2

THE WEIGHT

Use Suggested Strum Pattern #3
Moderately slow ♩ = 72

Intro:
N.C.

Words and Music by
ROBBIE ROBERTSON

And, and, and you put the load right on me.

Verse 2:
I picked up my bag, I went lookin' for a place to hide;
When I saw Carmen and the Devil walkin' side by side.
I said, "Hey, Carmen, come on, let's go downtown."
She said, "I gotta go, but my friend can stick around."
(To Chorus:)

Verse 3:
Go down, Miss Moses, there's nothin' you can say,
It's just ol' Luke, and Luke's waitin' on the Judgement Day.
"Well, Luke, my friend, what about young Anna Lee?"
He said, "Do me a favor, son, woncha stay an' keep Anna Lee company?"
(To Chorus:)

Verse 4:
Crazy Chester followed me, and he caught me in the fog.
He said, "I will fix your rack, if you'll take Jack, my dog."
I said, "Wait a minute, Chester, you know I'm a peaceful man."
He said, "That's okay, boy, won't you feed him when you can."
(To Chorus:)

Verse 5:
Catch a cannon ball now, to take me down the line.
My bag is sinkin' low and I do believe it's time.
To get back to Miss Fanny, you know she's the only one
Who sent me here with her regards for everyone.
(To Chorus:)

WHAT A FOOL BELIEVES

Use Suggested Strum Pattern #1
Moderately ♩ = 120

Words and Music by
KENNY LOGGINS and MICHAEL McDONALD

Intro:

He came from

Verse 1:

some-where back in her long ___ a - go, the sen - ti - men - tal fool don't see, try - in'

hard to re - cre - ate what had yet ___ to be cre - at - ed once in her life. ___ 2. She mus - ters a

Verses 2 & 3:

smile ___ for his nos - tal - gic tale, nev - er com - in' near what he want - ed to
some-where back in her long a - go, he can still be - lieve there's a place in her

say, ___ on - ly to re - al - ize it nev - er real - ly was. }
life, ___ some - day ___ some - where she will re - turn. }

Pre-chorus:

She had a place ___ in his life.

He nev - er made ___ her think twice. As he ris -

A WHITER SHADE OF PALE

Use Suggested Strum Pattern #5 or #1

Words and Music by
KEITH REID and GARY BROOKER

Moderately slow ♩ = 76

A Whiter Shade of Pale - 2 - 1

Verse 2:
She said, "There is no reason
And the truth is plain to see."
But I wandered through my playing cards,
And would not let her be
One of sixteen vestal virgins
Who were leaving for the coast.
And, although my eyes were open,
They might have just as well've been closed.
And so it was that later,
As the miller told his tale,
That her face, at first just ghostly,
Turned a whiter shade of pale.

A Whiter Shade of Pale - 2 - 2

WILD HORSES

Use Suggested Strum Pattern #3

Words and Music by
MICK JAGGER and KEITH RICHARDS

Wild Horses - 2 - 1

Verse 2:
I watched you suffer a dull aching pain.
Now you decided to show me the same.
No sweeping exits or offstage lines
Could make me feel bitter, or treat you unkind.
(To Chorus:)

Verse 3:
I know I dreamed you a sin and a lie.
I have my freedom, but I don't have much time.
Faith has been broken, tears must be cried.
Let's do some living after we die.
(To Chorus:)

WOODSTOCK

Moderately
Intro:
Use Suggested Strum Pattern #6

Words and Music by
JONI MITCHELL

1. Well, I came ___ ___ up-on ___ a child ___ of God, ___ he was walk-ing a - long ___ the road ___ and ___ I asked ___

2.3. See additional lyrics

___ him, "Tell me where are you go - ing?" this he told ___ me: said, "I'm go -

- ing down ___ to Yas - gur's Farm, ___ gon - na join ___ in a rock and roll ___ band. ___ Got to

get back ___ to the land ___ and set ___ my soul ___ free." We are star-

Chorus:

- dust, we are gold - en, we are bil - lion year old ___ car - bon, ___ and we got ___

___ to get ___ our - selves ___ back to the gar -

Repeat ad lib. & fade

1.2. **3.**

den. 2. Well, then den.

Verse 2:
Well, then can I walk beside you? I have come to lose the smog.
And I feel as if a cog in something turning.
And maybe it's the time of year, yes, and maybe it's the time of man.
And I don't know who I am but life is for learning.
(To Chorus:)

Verse 3:
By the time we got to Woodstock, we were half a million strong,
And everywhere was a song and a celebration.
And I dreamed I saw the bomber jet planes riding shotgun in the sky,
Turning into butterflies above our nation.
(To Chorus:)